Open Your

Heart

And Write Your

Vision

Regina Warren

ISBN 978-1-64569-363-5 (paperback)
ISBN 978-1-64569-364-2 (digital)

Christian Faith Publishing, Inc.
832 Park Avenue
Meadville, PA 16335
www.christianfaithpublishing.com

Printed in the United States of America

Contents

Creating a Clean Heart, It's A Heart Thang.....................................9

The Past, Let Go and Let God 13

I Am What He Says I Am, but Do You Believe It?.....................17

Jesus Is On The Main Line, Time To Pick Up 22

Recognize The Common Denominator and Break the Cycle........27

Thy Kingdom Come, Thy Will Be Done 32

The wilderness was a lonely place. I was searching for a peace that I could not find. I made up my mind to allow my broken pieces to be placed in the hands of the Manufacturer, my Lord and Savior.

If you are in a lonely place, this book is for you. I encourage you to make an appointment with the Manufacturer. With him as the center of your joy, you are given a peace that surpasses all understanding.

As you read, reflect, and meditate on these words, may you begin your journey of healing and become whole. You are an asset in the kingdom of God. My prayer is that God orders your steps as you write the vision God has for you and run with the confidence he planted in you. If you can see it and believe it, you most certainly can achieve it!

Lessons

Turn your wounds into wisdom.

—Oprah Winfrey

Creating a Clean Heart,
It's A Heart Thang

Do not conform to the pattern of this world,
but be transformed by the renewing of your mind.
Then you will be able to test and approve what God's will is,
his good, pleasing and perfect will.

—*Romans 12:2 (NIV)*

I t hurt. I know. I've been there. Heartbreak, stress, fear, worry, doubt, confusion, depression, insecurities, resentment, and brokenness. I could go on and on. I knew these things all too well. I decided to have "open heart surgery." I needed to identify the root cause of my heartaches and allow God to mend the broken pieces. It was a long but much needed procedure!

In order to begin the healing process, you must examine your heart. What you hold on to can keep you from moving forward! Take the time to process your emotions, the situation/circumstance, spend quality time in God's word/presence, and surround yourself with wise counsel. There are people who have been through what you are going through. They can hold your hand through your surgical procedure! My mother, pastor, and life coach helped me through, and they still do!

How you use the time to heal is what matters the most. You will have good days and bad days, but your best days are ahead of you! Transformation starts with taking a look at yourself. What happened to you, does not define you!

Reflection

Heart (noun) the central or innermost part of something; the vital part or essence

1) What heart issues are you holding on to?
2) Can you identify the origin of these heart issue(s)?
3) Who can you talk to or confide in?
4) There is an answer in the Manufacturer's manual (the Bible) that can treat your heart issues. Identify the truth found in God's word that addresses your heart issue(s) (e.g. worry, doubt, fear, rejection, abandonment). When these heart issues attempt to resurface, counter it with God's word!

Reflection Notes

"Heart Scriptures for Meditation"

Test me, Lord, and try me, examine my heart and my mind. (Psalm 26:2, NIV)

Take delight in the Lord, and he will give you the desires of your heart. (Psalm 37:4, NIV)

Create in me a pure heart, O God and renew a steadfast spirit within me. (Psalm 51:10, NIV)

Trust in the Lord with all you heart and lean not on your own understanding. (Proverbs 3:5, NIV)

Above all else, guard your heart, for everything you do flows from it. (Proverbs 4:23, NIV)

For where your treasure is, your heart will be also. (Matthew 6:21, NIV)

Peace I leave with you; my peace I give you. I do not give to you as the world gives. Do not let your hearts be troubled and do not be afraid. (John 14:27, NIV)

And the peace of God, which transcends all understanding, will guard your hearts and your minds in Christ Jesus. (Philippians 4:7, NIV)

The Past, Let Go and Let God

Brothers and sisters, I do not consider myself yet to have taken hold of it. But one thing I do: Forgetting what is behind and straining toward what is ahead, I press toward the goal to win the prize for which God has called me heavenward in Christ Jesus.

—Philippians 3:13 (NIV)

You're driving and constantly checking your rearview mirror. Why? You need to know what's behind you, right? You check your side mirrors to see if your past is creeping up on you. As you are heading to your new destination, don't get rerouted to past hurt, perceived failures, or other things that have come and gone! I don't know your situation, but I know you are searching for a new destination. Your desire is to leave the past behind, but you are apprehensive. You are in neutral, one gear shift closer to drive.

You have decided to let go and let God do a new thing in you. What does that new thing look like? Just as your car may need a tune up, oil change, transmission, or new tires, you too will have scheduled maintenance! The Manufacturer is ready to conduct your scheduled maintenance. God doesn't use our past against us. He uses it to show us that we are more than conquerors. Your tests, build your *Test*imony. It shows others that no matter the circumstance, God will meet you where you are. Your past is history! Now drive toward the place that God predestined for you!

Reflection

Past (adj.): gone by in time; no longer existing

1) Your past can keep you in spiritual/mental bondage *if* you allow it! What can you do to ensure you move forward?

Reflection Notes

But Lot's wife looked back, and she became a pillar of salt. (Genesis 19:26, NIV)

Jesus replied, "No one who puts a hand to the plow and looks back is fit for service in the kingdom of God." (Luke 9:62, NIV)

When I was a child, I talked like a child, I thought like a child, I reasoned like a child. When I became a man, I put the ways of childhood behind me. (1 Corinthians 13:11, NIV)

Therefore, if anyone is in Christ, the new creation has come; The old has gone, the new is here! (2 Corinthians 5:17, NIV)

Don't let anyone look down on you because you are young, but set an example or the believers in speech, in conduct, in love, in faith and in purity. (1 Timothy 4:12, NIV)

Anyone who listens to the word but does not do what it says is like someone who looks at his face in a mirror and, after looking at himself, goes away and immediately forgets what he looks like. (James 1:23–25, NIV)

It would have been better for them not to have known the way of righteousness, than to have known it and then to turn their backs on the sacred command that was passed on to them. "A sow that is washed returns to her wallowing in the mud." (2 Peter 2:21–22, NIV)

I Am What He Says I Am, but Do You Believe It?

I praise you because I am fearfully and wonderfully made;
your works are wonderful, I know that full well.

—*Psalm 139:14*

I was a superficial believer. I had a few scriptures memorized in order to mingle with the saints. You know, pretend. Praising him on the outside but feeding the desires of my flesh constantly. When times were good, so was God. When times were bad, I blamed God. I didn't know who God was. I didn't think he cared. The truth is, he does. I just didn't believe it.

The beautiful thing about our Manufacturer is that he created a package deal! We are unique individuals with God-given abilities, gifts, and talents given to us at birth. How wonderful is that? We are genuine gems. When we are lost, it is easy to forget who we are, and whose we are. That's what the enemy wants. The enemy wants to steal, kill, and destroy every fiber of your being.

How do you get to know who and whose you are? By spending quality time with your Manufacturer! *Believe God!* We were not built to break. We're strong, courageous, and *fearfully* and *wonderfully* made.

Reflection

Believe (verb): accept something as true

1) Does how you see yourself align with how God sees you?
2) Do you believe what God says about you?

Reflection Notes

So God created mankind in his own image, in the image of God he created them; male and female he created them. (Genesis 1:27, NIV)

For you created my inmost being, you knit me together in my mother's womb. (Psalm 139:13, NIV)

Your eyes saw my unformed body; all the days ordained for me were written in your book before one of them came to be. (Psalm 139:16, NIV)

And even the very hairs of your head are all numbered. So don't be afraid; you are worth more than many sparrows. (Matthew 10:30–31, NIV)

He predestined us for adoption to sonship through Jesus Christ, in accordance with his pleasure and will—to the praise of his glorious grace, which he has freely given us in the One he loves. (Ephesians 1:5–6, NIV)

Endure hardship as discipline; God is treating you as his children. For what children are not disciplined by their Father? If you are not disciplined, and everyone undergoes discipline, then you are not legitimate, not true sons and daughters at all. (Hebrews 12:7, NIV)

See what great love the Father has lavished on us, that we should be called children of God! And that is what we are! The reason the world does not know us is that it did not know him. Dear friends, now we are children of God, and what we will be has not yet been made known. But we know that when Christ appears, we shall be like him, for we shall see him as he is. (1 John 3:1–2, NIV)

Jesus Is On The Main Line, Time To Pick Up

*Then you will call on me and come and pray
to me, and I will listen to you.*

—Jeremiah 29:12

I t's easy for us to engage in conversations with friends, family, or co-workers when we are going through something. However, do we converse with God the same way? When things are going good our line is busy. When things are not going good we desire to talk to our Manufacturer and tell him what we desire. He already knows your heart, and he says in his Word that "No man knows the heart but me." There is nothing to hide. Stay on the main line, prayer will change things.

Reflection

Prayer (noun) a solemn request for help or expression of thanks addressed to God

1) When was the last time you had a soul session with God?
2) Prayer is an honest dialogue. Cherish how you communicate with the God and know he communicates with you too! He listens! Don't just pray for yourself, pray for others (family, friends, church leaders, heads of state, nations). After reading *Fervent: A Woman's Battle Plan for Serious,*

Specific, and Strategic Prayer, I incorporated the following prayer strategy:

Pray

P̲raise: Praise God and give thanks for what he has done
R̲epent: Acknowledge any wrongdoing, ask for forgiveness, and desire to turn away from it
A̲sk: Ask God for those things in his will
Y̲es: Know and believe that you will receive [1]

Prayers are answered in different ways. Be patient, your answer will come!

---

[1]   Shirer, P. (2015). Fervent: A Woman's Battle Plan for Serious, Specific, and Strategic Prayer. Nashville, TN: B&H Publishing Group.

Reflection Notes

If my people, who are called by my name, will humble themselves and pray and seek my face and turn from their wicked ways, then I will hear from heaven, and I will forgive their sin and will heal their land. (2 Chronicles 7:14, NIV)

You will pray to him, and he will hear you, and you will fulfill your vows. (Job 22:27, NIV)

He will respond to the prayer of the destitute; he will not despise their plea. (Psalm 102:17, NIV)

Watch and pray so that you will not fall into temptation. The spirit is willing, but the flesh is weak. (Matthew 26:41, NIV)

Therefore I tell you, whatever you ask for in prayer, believe that you have received it, and it will be yours. (Mark 11:24, NIV)

Be joyful in hope, patient in affliction, faithful in prayer. (Romans 12:12, NIV)

And pray in the Spirit on all occasions with all kinds of prayers and requests. With this in mind, be alert and always keep on praying for all the Lord's people. (Ephesians 6:18, NIV)

Do not be anxious about anything, but in every situation, by prayer and petition, with thanksgiving, present your requests to God. And the peace of God, which transcends all understanding, will guard your hearts and your mind in Christ Jesus. (Philippians 4:6–7, NIV)

Recognize The Common Denominator and Break the Cycle

You were taught, with regard to your former way of life,
to put off your old self which is being corrupted by its deceitful desires;
to be made new in the attitude of your minds; and to put on the
new self, created to be like God in true righteousness and holiness.

—Ephesians 4:22–24

The definition of insanity is doing the same thing over and over, expecting different results. Insanity was impacting my sanity! I had to change my actions if I wanted different results. I had to identify the common denominators that kept me recycling negative habits. In math a common denominator is when two or more fractions have the same number at the bottom. In life we have common denominators such as habits, behaviors, actions, and feelings that either help us grow or hinder us.

Some common denominators for me were people pleasing, unhealthy relationships, low self-esteem, faking it until I could make it, not letting go of the past, anger, idols, and unforgiveness. These things kept me from healing and working toward becoming a whole person. Recognizing your common denominator is key. Today is the day you resign from waste management and stop recycling common denominators.

Reflection

Cycle (noun): A series of events that are repeated in the same order

1) What is/are your common denominator/s?
2) How can you break the cycle?

Reflection Notes

Discretion will protect you, and understanding will guard you. Wisdom will save you from men whose words are perverse. (Proverbs 2:11–12, NIV)

Why do you look at the speck of sawdust in your brother's eye and pay no attention to the plank in your own eye? How can you say to your brother, "Let me take the speck out of your eye," when all the time there is a plank in your own eye? You hypocrite, first take the plank out of your own eye, and then you will see clearly to remove the speck from our brother's eye. (Matthew 7:3–5, NIV)

No good tree bears bad fruit, nor does a bad tree bear good fruit. Each tree is recognized by its own fruit. People do not pick figs from thorn bushes or grapes from briers. (Luke 6:43–44, NIV)

No temptation has overtaken you except what is common to mankind. And God is faithful; he will not let you be tempted beyond what you can bear. (1 Corinthians 10:13, NIV)

Do not be deceived, bad company ruins good morals. (1 Corinthians 15:33, NIV)

And give no opportunity to the devil. (Ephesians 4:27, NIV)

For we do not wrestle against flesh and blood, but against the authorities, against the cosmic powers over this present darkness, against the spiritual forces of evil in the heavenly places. (Ephesians 6:12, NIV)

Finally, brothers, whatever is true whatever is honorable whatever is just whatever is pure, whatever is lovely, whatever is commendable, if there is anything worthy of praise, think about these things. (Philippians 4:8, NIV)

Thy Kingdom Come,
Thy Will Be Done

For I know the plans I have for you, declares the Lord,
plans to prosper you and not to harm you,
plans to give you hope and a future. Then you will call on me
and come and pray to me, and I will listen to you.

—Jeremiah 29:11

God has a plan for you. You have a divine assignment that *must* be completed. Yes, assignment. Jesus had an assignment! God is going to use you, your gifts, and your experiences for his glory. Your journey is unique to you. Sharing your experiences with the world can help someone get through and over! Every tear that was shed, prayer that was prayed, and obstacle that you broke through prepared you for your break through.

There was a purpose for the pain. You endured the battle so you can complete the assignment. You have everything you need to complete your assignment because you acquired many tools (life lessons and experiences) along the way.

Reflection

Plan (noun): An intention or decision about what one is going to do

1) Your assignment is bigger than you! It's the footprint that you leave in the world. Whether you touch one life or several lives, you have left an impression. Just like Jesus left an impression in our lives. What do you believe is God's plan for you?
2) How will what you've gone through help someone get through?

Reflection Notes

It was good for me to be afflicted so that I might learn your decrees. (Psalm 119:71, NIV)

Trust in the Lord with all your heart and lean not on your own understanding; in all your ways submit to him, and he will make your paths straight. (Proverbs 3:5–6, NIV)

He has shown you, O mortal, what is good. And what does the Lord require of you? To act justly and to love mercy and to walk humbly with your God. (Micah 6:8, NIV)

Then he said to them all: "Whoever wants to be my disciple must deny themselves and take up their cross daily and follow me." (Luke 9:23, NIV)

Be very careful, then, how you live not as unwise but as wise, making the most of every opportunity, because the days are evil. (Ephesians 5:15–16, NIV)

Give thanks in all circumstances; for this is God's will for you in Christ Jesus. (1 Thessalonians 5:18, NIV)

You need to persevere so that when you have done the will of God, you will receive what he has promised. (Hebrews 10:36, NIV)

The Lord is not slow in keeping his promise, as some understand slowness. Instead he is patient with you, not wanting anyone to perish, but everyone to come to repentance. (2 Peter 3:9, NIV)

Blessings

We may encounter many defeats, but we must not be defeated.

—Maya Angelou

And the Lord answered me, write the vision, make it
plain on tablets, so he may run who reads it.

—Habakkuk 2:2 (NIV)

Y ou're taking the first step toward charting your path of success! Writing *your* vision. This journey will not be easy, but
I promise it will be worth it. This visionary strategic action
plan for success will help you make your vision come to fruition!
Writing your vision is a three-step process:

1) *See It*—See your vision by constructing a vision board that
   aligns with short-term and long-term goals.
2) *Believe It*—God has and will provide everything you need
   along your purposeful path (mentors, opportunities for
   personal/professional growth and development, resources,
   etc.).
3) *Achieve It*—Have a strategic action plan to press toward
   your goals.

Review your visionary plan monthly or quarterly to make sure
you are on track. If you suffer from procrastination, like myself, get
an accountability partner! Trust me, it helps when you have someone
who will hold you accountable.

Whether your goals are in the areas of health, wealth, relationships, career, or faith, utilize this plan as a blueprint for building a
solid foundation for your future. *You can do this*! Will it be challeng-
ing? Yes. Will you want to quit? Absolutely. Get out of your own way!
What's the worst that can happen? You fail? Well, I have news for
you, success is the formal attire of failure! It's time to *write your vision*!

Vision Statement

Vision

The ability to think about or plan the future with imagination or wisdom; a mental image of what the future will or could be like. Close your eyes and envision the life you desire to have. What does it look like? What are you doing? Who are you helping? What have you achieved?

Write your vision below.

_____

_____

_____

_____

_____

_____

_____

_____

_____

_____

_____

_____

_____

_____

_____

_____

_____

_____

_____

_____

Let's Be S.M.A.R.T. About It

The S.M.A.R.T goal and objective concept was developed by George Doran. The S.M.A.R.T. model helps managers develop concrete goals, and objectives for organizations (Doran, 1981). Just like organizations have goals, so do you! So let's be S.M.A.R.T. about it, and create a strategic action plan for success.

What does the S.M.A.R.T. acronym mean?

Specific—Targets a specific area

Measurable—What evidence shows that the goal was achieved? How often will you complete tasks associated with the goal?

Attainable—Assess if you have the knowledge, skills, and abilities to achieve the goal.

Relevant—Does the goal align with your overall vision for health, wealth, education, college plans, career plan, relationships, etc.

Time bound—A time frame or deadline for the goal to be achieved.[2]

---

[2] Doran, G. T (1981). There's a S.M.A.R.T. Way to Write Management's Goals and Objectives. AMA Forum

Example:

Goal: Create and publish *Write the Vision Strategic Action Plan Workbook* by December 31.

Specific: Write the Vision Strategic Action Plan

Measurable: If the planner is created and published by December 31

Attainable: I don't have the knowledge or skills yet, but I am looking at opportunities to acquire the knowledge and skills needed.

Relevant: This planner aligns with my vision to help others strategically plan for their future

Time bound: December 31

Goals generally fall into five categories:

Faith
Relationship
Health
Wealth
Career

What goals do you desire to achieve? What action steps are you going to take to achieve them? The time is now, use the next few pages to write out your goals! "Let's Be S.MA.R.T. About It."

"Let's Be S.M.A.R.T About It"

Faith

GOAL #1:

GOAL #2:

GOAL #3:

GOAL #4:

GOAL #5:

"Let's Be S.M.A.R.T About It"

Career

GOAL #1:

GOAL #2:

GOAL #3:

GOAL #4:

GOAL #5:

"Let's Be S.M.A.R.T About It"

Wealth

GOAL #1:

GOAL #2:

GOAL #3:

GOAL #4:

GOAL #5:

"Let's Be S.M.A.R.T About It"

Health

GOAL #1:

GOAL #2:

GOAL #3:

GOAL #4:

GOAL #5:

"Let's Be S.M.A.R.T About It"

Relationships

GOAL #1:

GOAL #2:

GOAL #3:

GOAL #4:

GOAL #5:

S.W.O.T. Analysis

Now in order for you to get where you are going, you need to assess where you are! We are going to examine four areas:

Strengths—A strong attribute or inherent asset. What are you good at (i.e. organization, budgeting, photography, social media, giving advice to friends, study habits, encouraging people)?

Weakness—Lacking skill or proficiency (i.e. receiving constructive criticism, asking for help, discipline, procrastination, laziness, self-control, being consistent)

Opportunities—a good chance for advancement or progress (i.e. scholarships, freelance work, professional networks, clubs/organizations, volunteering, workshops)

Threats—To cause to feel insecure or anxious (i.e. yourself fear, worry, doubt, your friendship circle) so that you can recognize it when it appears and have a strategy to combat it.[3]

On the next page, you will conduct a S.W.O.T. Analysis!

---

[3]   Merriam-Webster's Collegiate Dictionary. (1999). [10th Edition]. Springfield, MA: Merriam-Webster Incorporated.

S.W.O.T. Analysis

Strengths:

_____
_____
_____
_____
_____
_____
_____
_____
_____
_____
_____
_____
_____
_____

Weakness (areas of improvement):

_____
_____
_____
_____
_____
_____
_____
_____
_____
_____
_____
_____
_____
_____

S.W.O.T. Analysis

Opportunities:

_____
_____
_____
_____
_____
_____
_____
_____
_____
_____
_____
_____
_____
_____
_____

Threats:

_____
_____
_____
_____
_____
_____
_____
_____
_____
_____
_____
_____
_____
_____
_____

Mentoring

Mentoring is defined as a professional relationship with an experienced person. If there is a specific area in your life that you desire to grow, get a mentor! A mentor can narrow your focus, help you through the peaks and valleys of life, and be your accountability partner. Who can mentor you in the areas below? (You don't have to list someone for each category)

Faith:

_____

_____

_____

Career:

_____

_____

_____

Health:

_____

_____

_____

Wealth:

_____

_____

_____

Relationships:

_____

_____

_____

Affirmations

Your vision will be tested for authenticity. Write down ten affirmations or scriptures that will get you through those difficult times.

Examples:

—I will achieve my goal and overcome any obstacle that comes my way.
—I am fearfully and wonderfully made.

_____

_____

_____

_____

_____

_____

_____

_____

_____

_____

_____

_____

_____

_____

_____

_____

_____

_____

_____

_____

_____
_____
_____
_____
_____
_____
_____
_____
_____
_____
_____
_____

Word/Phrase for the Year

Ex: Shifting, Growth, Breaking Chains, Victorious

_____

Definition of word or explain how the motivational phrase relates to your vision

_____
_____
_____
_____
_____
_____
_____
_____
_____
_____
_____

Visionary Achievement Agreement

I, _____, have accepted the
charge to write my vision. I hold myself accountable for this visionary plan. I see this plan, I believe this plan, and I will achieve this
plan.

_____

Signature

_____

Date

_____

Accountability Partner Signature (optional)

_____

Date

Buckle up, Visionary, it's going to be a ride to remember. As you embark upon your journey toward clear vision, watch out for distractions that will offer alternate routes!

Anytime you need a reminder of who you are, whose you are, and where you are headed, open this book and remember you were not built to break!

---

4 Write The Vision "See It, Believe It, Achieve It" LLC (2018). Visionary Action Plan

About the Author

D r. Regina Warren is the founder of Write The Vision "See It, Believe It, Achieve It" LLC, which helps individuals turn their dreams into a strategic action plan. Dr. Warren loves encouraging individuals to achieve their hearts' desires and tap into their God-given potential! She has conducted "Envision Your Vision" vision board workshops educating individuals on the S.M.A.R.T. goal concept, strategic planning, and vision board construction. She continues to spread motivation via her YouTube Channel: WTV Monday Motivation. She believes if you can see and believe your vision, you most certainly can achieve it!

CPSIA information can be obtained
at www.ICGtesting.com
Printed in the USA
BVHW021145181019
561494BV00015B/102/P